Life, Death, And Everything In Between

Rheanna Ann Jikku

BookLeaf Publishing

Presentation by *BookLeaf Publishing*

Web: www.bookleafpub.com

E-mail: info@bookleafpub.com

ISBN: 9789360945091

First edition 2023

For my sisters, thanks for the help

ACKNOWLEDGEMENT

I would like to thank my family for all their encouragement. I thank my sisters for being my proofreaders and telling me to trust my abilities. My gratitude to my parents for reminding me and encouraging me to nurture my poetry. Finally, I appreciate my friends for reading my poetry as soon as I wrote it in the middle of class.

The Glass Dancer

I once met a girl
With skin as delicate as glass
Trapped in a theatre
Where no time would pass

She would dance around in circles
Her dancing shoes tied in a knot
They were dusty and worn
As if they were used a lot

I would watch her every night in my dreams
In a dirty little theatre seat
As she twirled around on the stage
On her quick lithe feet

I used to ask her endlessly
Why she would dance
She would never give me an answer
Her mind stuck in a trance

One day, she looked into my eyes
And told me a story
Of a girl piled with expectations
And the need for glory

She spoke of walking into the woods
Near a place one would call her home
And rain pelted on her coat
As she ran away from home

She spoke of losing a competition
And facing her parents' disappointment,
That they expressed their problems
On her in an angry vent

She had had enough
Of their endless issues
And she ended up in between tall trees
A dilemma made by many fools

She wandered amongst the trunks
Before she found an old lady
Sitting on a rotting tree stump
Which she found a little crazy

The lady led her to this buiding
And said she could stay here
But it came with a condition
That she accepted with no fear

I asked her what the condition was
And she said, her voice melancholy
That she should perform
On the stage for all of eternity

But she had stopped to tell me the story
And when I questioned why
She smiled tiredly
And on the stage she lies

Slowly, her eyes closed
And her body shimmered out of existence
It happened both slow and fast
It felt as if I was looking through a camera lens

I woke up the next day
My heart heavy with a smile that felt sadder
And I swore never to forget
The story of the glass dancer

Memories

The sound of rain
That's all she hears
The pitter-patter of raindrops
Is all that reaches her ears

She remembers when she was young
She would play in the rain with her brother
She would run out without an umbrella
And after, get scolded by mother.

As she remembers, crimson blood leaks
From the gunshot wound she received
The scarlet liquid mixing with water
As she lay on the concrete desolate

As her last breath abandons her lungs
And as her last tears fall
She remembers all the memories
That were accompanied by rainfall

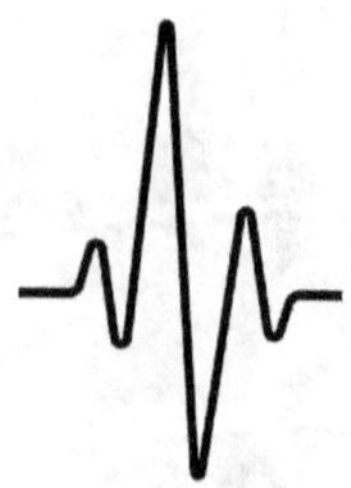

Those Birthday Thoughts

The thought felt weird
The one of not existing
Of not being there anymore
Of eventually losing everything.

From their memories,
Would we slowly disappear?
Or would it be so quick
With no one shedding a tear

What would be left
Once our earthly achievements are gone
Would we be just forgotten
The moment fate's scissors are drawn

When the feats you had gotten,
When the people who loved you faded away,
From their memories, just a voice remains
Or just the thought of one silly childhood play.

Where would you go
Once you leave this earth?
Would it be to a place in your memories
Or into another birth

Pulled back into the present
With a birthday cake in front of me.
With the people I love surrounding me
I decided not to worry

As I put aside the thoughts
The ones that whirl in my head
Enjoying the moment of life I am in
Not caring about anything too far ahead

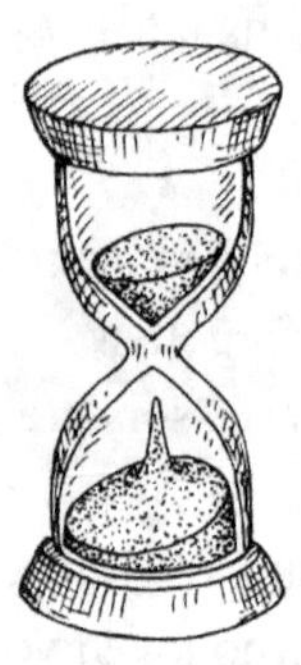

Betrayal

For as long as I remember
I've seen those caring eyes.
That sweet, melancholy smile
And gangly clothes much too oversized.

But those once beautiful eyes
Stared back at me, silently
And I gazed upon in shock,
As I was stabbed violently.

There's no more kind smile,
Only a crooked sneer
And she twisted a knife painfully
As from my eyes, spilled a tear.

My eyes seemed to question
On why the betrayal so cheap.
Her smirk had answered
Because you trusted so deep.

The blade was pulled out
And velvet blood started to flow,
As I fell to the ground
I wondered from when her love was for show.

She looked down at my grief-filled body
And walked away, without any regret.
My eyes closed painfully, for the last time,
As my thoughts went to someone I wished I
never met.

Silent

The stars grow bright
As the girl looks up
They look like white paint on black
Like drops of water from a cup

The snow makes the stars blurry
As it was a heavy winterfall
And the girl tears up
As she curls up into a ball

She thinks back a few hours
To when she strayed
From the usual path she takes
Even though the sky had greyed

She had seen the snow get heavier
And turned back but to her dismay
The path had been covered with snow
And she had lost her way

The sky grows darker
As the cold takes air from her
As her body is enveloped by numbness
And everything becomes a blur

The next morn, her parents found
Her cold body with snow all around
And they mourned and they grieved
As she lay silent on the ground

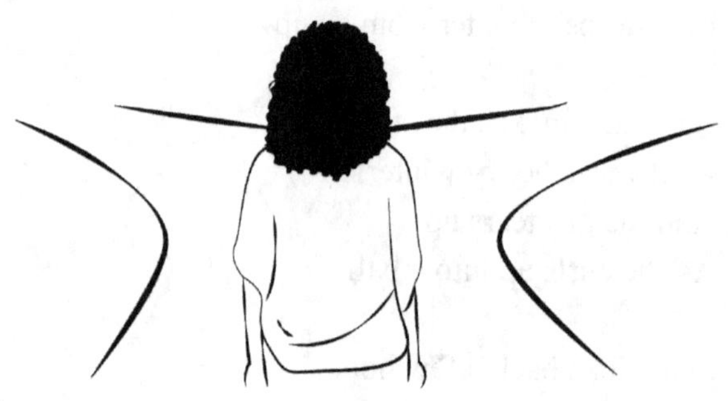

Flame To Fire

The world is bright
That is undeniable
With fires and flames
That were so very unreliable

Some used to nurture
To give warmth and comfort,
And some used to harm
Burning the mightiest fort.

What had occurred
To bring about the act of harming?
An angry burnt life
Over something so charming

From a life of peace using flames,
To one filled with burnt-down forests.
From homes being filled with sweet heat
To fire bringing people to a forceful rest

It was a question
That was answered long ago
Because humans grew selfish
Growing a big ego

So as the world moves on
And humans with it
What should be remembered most of all
How flames have changed quite a bit

Peek-a-boo

As I sat on my bed
With work to do
I heard a voice
Going peek-a-boo.

I froze for a moment
My limbs going numb
Aiming to ignore it,
A decision that was oh so dumb.

Later I would see
From the corner of my vision,
A figure at my window
Looking my way with precision.

Turning my head in its direction
Finding nothing through the glass,
I sighed a breath of relief
Moving to continue my work for class.

Turning off the lights
As I finished my classwork,
Looking around in the darkness
I see a shadow lurk.

I hastily shut my eyes
My blanket now moved over my head,
And hoped it was my imagination
Though my heart filled with dread.

I was almost asleep when suddenly
A hand tugged my leg,
Pulling me off my bed,
As I smelt the scent of nutmeg.

My heart pounded in my chest
As my blanket slipped off my face
And to my horror, I saw
A dark figure dressed in bloodstained lace.

It had no discernable features
And sharp claws on each hand,
With a huge jarring smile,
With eyes both hard and bland.

It scratched me on my neck
And in my vision, darkness passed through.
Hearing near my ear
An eery voice saying Peek-a-boo.

Under the sea

The sea is beautiful
With its colours
And with its waves
Pushing and pulling for hours

Even now, as I lay under
The sea I found so pretty
I still have the same thoughts
Drowning from an idea I thought was witty

The story goes as most might
With a dare to start it all
An unnecessary chain of event
And a price that was so very tall

We were on a boat
My dear friends and I
The waves were higher than usual
Though no one thought to wonder why

We were playing truth or dare
And it was dare I foolishly picked
I had to jump into the frigid water
Something that would lead to my end

I had lept into the water
Freezing and yelling expletives
The cold in my body
Going off like explosives

As I moved back to the ladder
Near the boat's other side
The horrifying happen
A wave pulled me away, its grasp wide

I found myself under the water
Not knowing what is up and down
Panicking, I swam in a random direction
As I slowly started to drown

Breaching the surface for a slight second
Managing to breathe in some air
A wave pulled me back down
A childish part in my brain thinking, "unfair"

I heard my friends' screams
Although they were garbled
Shouting out my name
From my throat, the air bubbled

I lost the little air I had
As the seconds go by
The thought of dying scared me
That I would not lie

Death came quicker than I thought
I slowly lost consciousness
As my lungs filled with water
And my vision filled with darkness

The water was always mesmerising
As it sparkled and shined
The thought of my stupidity
Flashed through my mind

A Petty Crime

Tears wouldn't have stopped it,
Something I've heard repeatedly.
It wouldn't have stopped the blood spilling
Nor the sirens blaring loudly.

But they kept flowing
At the thought of red-stained shoes,
At the sight of her clothes
Or the scent of her shampoos.

We were walking home
From the dreariness of school.
"Take a shortcut" she said
And I thought she was so cool.

The "shortcut" was dark
An alley that was long,
Yet my friend shouldered on
Me being forced to follow along.

It happened so quickly
But it remained in my mind,
We were nearing the end of the alley
When destiny decided to not be kind.

Someone came out of the shadows,
A person with a gun in hand
And threatened us for money
Shooting a bullet near where we stand.

Scared for what would happen
We gave up the money we had
And we're relieved as I backed away
Thinking we were out of the bad.

Though that was not what happened
As he aimed his gun straight at us
And swiftly released a bullet
Running away without any fuss.

The deadly shot had found its target
Straight into my friend's chest.
I screamed for help as she fell
Help only arriving after she was put to rest.

Everything after was a blur
The ambulance and the hospital check.
I was lost in a mournful haze
Because there was no pulse on her neck.

The funeral was planned they said
To happen in two days' time.
As I thought of my friend,
The victim to a petty crime.

Revenge I Took

All I wanted to say
What was one way to say I hate you?
To say you are the worst?
To say the feeling was not new?

The thoughts roam my mind
As I look into your eyes
And I see your carefree smile
Knowing it's all lies

I always think of that day
When I found out about the betrayal
When I saw the eye-opening video
That I can remember without fail

In the security camera, I had seen
You and the shot fired
Straight at my sister
Changing how my brain was wired

I remember hearing the news
From you nonetheless
About how she was shot
You looked to be in so much stress

I mourned with you
Over the once-thought-shared loss
Was it something you had planned
Or a random coin toss?

Was she collateral damage
Or had something happened?
To make you shoot her
In a journal, I had this penned

As you looked at me
Not a bit of guilt in your gaze
I doubled down in my plan
My eyes filled in with a vengeful blaze

Walking down a deserted road
I quietly pulled out a knife
You hadn't noticed
Looking as if all was good in your life

I slowed down a bit
You walking in front of me
Before stabbing it in your back
My mind in a calculated glee

You turned to me in shock
And fell on the ground
I crouched down next to you
Happy at the damage I found

As you lost your last few breathes
I whispered that I knew
Pulling out my knife
Blood staining the knife once new

I walked away from the body
Later dumping the blade in a river
I would always think gladly
About the revenge I took for my sister

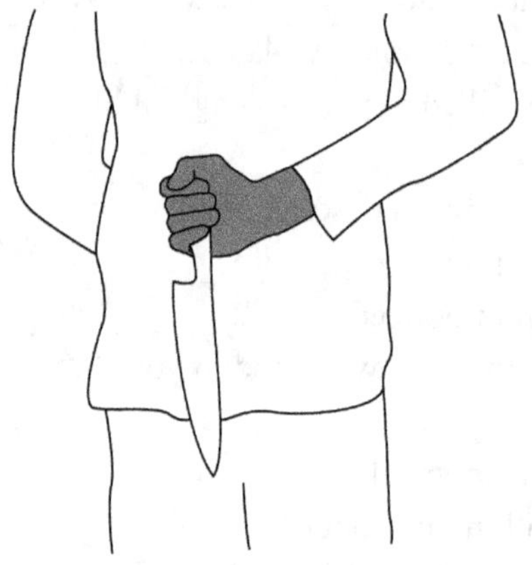

The Sunset

It was majestic, wasn't it?
The sight of the waves
Mowing back and front on the beach,
A bit of the sand, it shaves.

As we sit on a grassy patch
Some ways away from the sand,
We watch as the waves meeting the beach
And as water collides with land.

We'd been sitting there for a while
Admiring the horizon quietly.
Not a single sound we uttered,
A moment without any of life's anxiety.

I turned to look at you
Your face still towards the sea.
Your eyes a reflection of the water,
The bluest of blues to me.

The setting sun shined on your skin
A beautiful sight to witness.
Your hair flopping around you
For all of your calm stillness.

You turn towards me,
Finally noticing my eyes on you,
And smiled at me,
It was such a pretty view.

Turning back to the sea
Our hands at a finger's reach.
I swore to always remember
The sunset at the beach.

Fairytales and Fireflies

Fairytales and fireflies
Always were her favourite things.
Fireflies with their light
And fairytales of people with wings.

She remembers when she was younger,
Nothing but a mere child,
When she could not sleep
Her parents just smiled.

They would take out a book
Old and unassuming
But filled with majestic tales
Of their own choosing.

They would go through their backdoor
Settling on their cosy porch
With blankets and pillows they brought
And a lamp with an artificial torch.

Her parents would take turns reading
Out of the brown book
And fireflies would slowly light
As their flight they took.

She remembered looking in wonder
At the sight of the fireflies,
At their coincidental patterns
As they moved through the skies.

She remembered her parents' words
As they went through the tales
With silly voices and avid descriptions
Of pirates with their sturdy sails.

On a silent lonely night,
In her own little house,
She had found the big book,
A crinkle between her brows.

She had thought why not
And went out to her backyard.
Curled up in her blanket,
Fingers tracing where the book was marred.

She picked out a random story
Reading it with interest
Enjoying the little memories
Of her with her parents in their little nest.

After finishing the story
And finally looking up she saw
The light of fireflies
She stared in awe.

She watched them for a while
And their calming flying motions,
She read another story
Of a witch and her potions.

Feeling tired and relaxed
She went back into her home.
On her bedside she placed
Her nostalgia-inducing tome.

As she slept, she dreamt
Of the wonders she saw with her eyes
And her nights would be filled
With fairytales and fireflies.

Movie Night

The lights were low and soothing,
The sounds not too loud.
His clothes felt crumpled
Much more so than he usually allowed.

In his apartment, he lay
Unsure of how this occurred,
How this had developed?
The drinks making his mind obscured.

The night started out simply
Just a night in with some friends.
They cooked dinner and relaxed,
The drinks coming out in the end.

A couple drinks in
And they wanted to watch a movie.
Settling on the couch,
A decision between Lion King and Judge Judy.

They argued for a while
With objections such as these:
'Judge Judy isn't a movie!'
And 'we don't want no Disney!'

He watched in silent amusement
As neither wanted to lose.
Abruptly his friends asked him in unison
For him to choose.

Taking the remote silently,
Leaving his friends blind,
He scrolled through Netflix
And started playing Megamind.

His friends begrudgingly settled.
On the ground he sat,
And he looked at his friends
The blanket under him he pat.

Halfway through the movie,
Two arms wrapped around him.
He just shrugged and continued to try drink
A glass with water filled to the brim.

As the credits of the movie rolled,
He offed the tv while his eyes slowly closed.
The movie night was nice he thought
As he joined his friends as they dozed.

Heavy Is The Head

She never wanted this
The extravagant gowns and balls,
The lengthy meetings that didn't matter,
The servants running through the halls.

She would rather be anywhere else
Not trapped in walls empty and plain.
Filled with manners of expensive items
The bleakness driving her insane.

Somedays she would hear whispers,
Echoing through the palace
Of the adventures of pirates
Spoken with such malice.

Though, she would find herself wondering
More often than not,
If her life were any different
Could it be her searching for the next gold pot?

She would sometimes imagine
Her life as a baker
Or how nice it would be
To be the daughter of a shoemaker.

She knew that she was ungrateful
Her path of life so sure,
But she couldn't help it
The day of her coronation growing closer.

She had never wanted the responsibilities
Or the pressure to be perfect.
To rub elbows with the obnoxious,
To know matters of every subject.

As the cursed day arrived,
She was resigned to her fate
And held her shoulders straight
As she accepted the crown so ornate.

As the years passed by
And she became the cold queen,
Ruthless and powerful
Though rarely ever seen.

As she slowly wastes away her days
Maintaining her kingdom with an ever-present
frown,
She thought of a saying she read long ago
Heavy is the head that wears the crown.

One Last Dance

We were just two kids
With a whole life ready for us.
With nothing to worry,
Our lives together we would discuss.

One day was all it took
To take you away from me,
To rip a part of my heart away
Even as I would plea.

One stupid drunk driver
Who basically got off scot-free.
We were in the car together
Leaving me to question why you, not me?

The days after were a blur,
My mind a scrambled mess.
The funeral was solemn,
My face not showing my distress.

I lay in my room
Unable to control my sobbing,
When music starts from my phone
And I sit up, my head throbbing.

I recognize the song,
The one we would always play.
Us clumsily waltzing around the room,
Making my thoughts fray.

I could almost see the outlines
Of us swaying around,
Tripping over each other feet,
Eventually, we would fall to the ground.

My mind in a delirious haze,
I found myself rising
Off the lumpy bed
With the just memory of us dancing.

Moving my hands into the air,
My face still in disorder,
I slowly start moving
Through my room with no order.

I could almost see you in front of me,
Your face laughing as we stumbled,
Your laughter echoing around,
I could feel it in my heart as it rumbled.

The song was about to end
And my parents find me engrossed,
Wobbling mindlessly, alone in my room
As I savoured one last dance.

A Modern-Day Romeo And Juliet

Tiptoeing through alleys,
Not a single sound had been made
As I thought about how the night turned out,
Filled with memories sure to not fade.

It started as all others had
Ever since my eyes found yours,
With me sneaking to your house
Not stopping to make any detours.

Jumping over your fence
And ensuring to make the thud of my feet silent.
Climbing the willow tree near your window,
In my hands the branches were pliant.

Reaching your room and knocking on the glass
twice,
My mind anticipating talking to you finally
And seeing your smile as you open your window,
The room behind you showcasing your family's
refinery.

Spending the night together,
Until too quick, the sun started to rise.
Talking about anything and everything
As I admired your ethereal beauty with my own
two eyes.

As I was about to leave through the window,
As we had before to avoid your father and mother,
Not yet ready to depart
Our arms wrapped around each other.

Enjoying the warmth the hug gave me
For way too little time
Before we heard movement,
Frozen as if we were caught in a crime.

Letting go of each other with a kiss
As I climbed out of the window,
Back to my antiquated house I went,
Thinking of the moment with you that no one
would know.

Back in my bed, I thought of our dilemma,
Like those old stories of a love so private
Of two who could never be together,
Like a modern-day Romeo and Juliet.

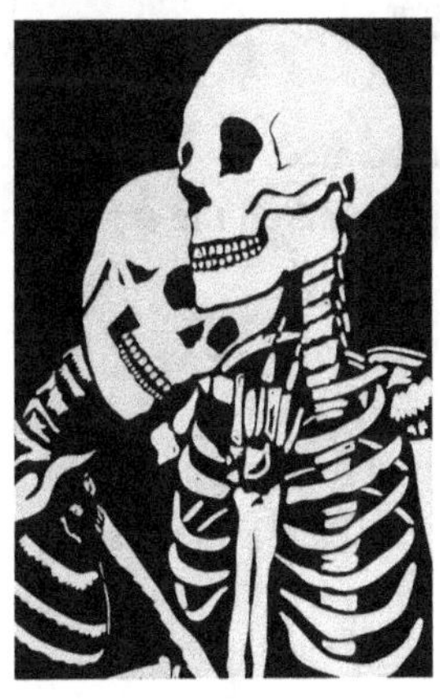

The Feathery Hat

As I sat on the ground, I spoke,
"You remember that hat,
The one with the absurd colours,
The one that made you look as crazy as a bat."

"Well I do, the hat at the thrift store,
I remember when you first saw it
And fell in love with the feathers,
Looking as if it was made with a DIY kit."

"That day, you weren't able to get it.
Pockets empty, just window shopping we had
said.
We had come back the next day
But we couldn't find it in the thrift store's
vibrant spread."

"After what happened, I was a mess
And had blindly walked the store,
Just to see it on a rack
Where we hadn't checked before."

After buying it and going home,
I had noticed the tears I could see through.

I fixed them up with a thread and needle
And now it will be finally given to you."

I smile sadly with tears welling up
As I finished my story.
I pushed myself onto my knees,
Looking at the grave before me.

I placed the hat on the slab,
Its brightness was an eyesore.
Placing a rock on top of the hat,
So that to the sky, it wouldn't soar.

Laying a bouquet in front of the grave,
I stood up, dusting my knees.
Even as I slowly walked out of the graveyard,
I could still see the feathery hat with ease.

Rendezvous

Every morning, you would run up to me,
Your expression smiley and happy,
As you would talk about your lover and your
sweet rendezvous
Then groan about how you were being sappy.

You would talk about how you two would meet
nightly
At the rooftop of our apartment building,
That you would talk until sunrise,
Your voice would be sweetly lilting.

I would listen in smiling sadly
As chattered about your night to anyone near
And I knew the whispers our neighbour would
mutter,
The ones you seemingly never hear.

I knew what had happened
A tragic event a month ago,
Of an accident in front of the building
And a body lying in red snow.

Snapping out of my thoughts I could see
You still going on about your night,
About how you danced with your lover,
Holding each other tight.

Every night, without fail,
I would see you walk up the apartment stairs,
Knowing you would be smiling in a slight daze,
To the roof upstairs.

One day, I went up the steps,
A few minutes before midnight,
Intending to tell you the truth,
But meeting a melancholy sight.

You were lying on the cold ground
As you giggled and pointed out different stars.
You were smoking carefree
In your hand was a lit cigar.

I yearned to tell the truth,
That they were gone but like a buffoon,
I had remained quiet,
Watching as you talk to the moon.

The Light In The House

The light grew bright in his house
Noticed the boy alarmed,
And the flames grew bigger
As he stood on the sidewalk, forever scarred.

His legs moved on their own
In to his burning home
To save his family
Who were trapped in the fiery dome.

He had thought he could save them,
But soon realised he was wrong
As he heard loud wails
That reverberated in his head with a gong

He looked in despair
At his parents' lifeless bodies,
At his mother's once smiling face,
At his father's blank eyes.

The boy heard a cry
And froze, eyes wide
As he ran up the stairs
To where his baby sister lied.

He opened the door fearful
But to his horror he saw,
His sister so dear
On the floor with her face raw.

She cried still holding
To the hope of a life that would not come,
And as her final breath left her, he gave up
Sitting down and surrendering to where he came
from.

The Butterfly and You

The sounds aren't loud,
The colours not too bright,
Lying on the grass
And inhaling the sweet air of the night.

The smell of the trees
Wafting through the clearing.
Woodland creatures making little noises,
A scene from a movie in the making.

You're right next to me,
Staring at the stars with a smile.
Your vision edged by the tips of trees
As if putting the sight in a memory file.

Out of all the beauty in that moment
The only thing that catches my eye
Is the face you make,
Nose scrunching at the sight of a butterfly.

Floating through the area,
A break from the endless green
Without a care in the world
Wings cast with a silver sheen.

As you raise up your hand
And tried to get the butterfly to sit
For just a second on your finger,
My heart takes a heavy hit.

As if taking pity on you
With the gleam of joy in your eyes,
The butterfly lands on your finger
Its wings the colour of the brightest dyes.

That second, I experienced
A sight that was caught by few,
Of the moon shining brightly
On the butterfly and you.

End Of Time

At the end of time,
All things living shall stop.
The world will watch
As the rivers swamp.

And the sky shall fall
With the stars twinkling out,
And the earth crumbling quickly
Faster than any could count.

The world will mourn
As their last seconds tick away
And the moon will be full
On its last journey in the day.

The deserts will flood
And the oceans will dry.
The planets will wilt
And the animals die.

Civilisations will burn
From the same pollution it caused
And as the fire grows,
All would have watched.

As the last breath goes out
At the end of time,
The souls shall weep
As they watch the world filled with grime.

* 9 7 8 9 3 6 0 9 4 5 0 9 1 *